Chihuahua

Señor Tiny

by Natalie Lunis

Consultant: Patricia Larrissey
Chihuahua Breeder and Exhibitor

BEARPORT
PUBLISHING

New York, New York

Credits

Cover and Title Page, © Annette Shaff; TOC, © mpikula mpikula/Istockphoto; 4, © Eric Bellamy 2007; 5, © Joel Sartore/National Geographic/Getty Images; 6, © Eric Bellamy 2007; 7T, © Eric Bellamy 2007; 7B, © Eric Bellamy 2007; 8T, © North Carolina Museum of Art/Corbis; 8B, © Colima half-lying Dog, 300 BC - 500 BC (ceramic), Colima Culture/Museo Amparo, Puebla, Mexico, Jean-Pierre Courau/The Bridgeman Art Library; 9T, © aerialarchives.com/Alamy; 9B, © Montezuma, the Emperor of Mexico (1466-1520) 1780 (coloured engraving), Duflos, Pierre (1742-1816)/Private Collection, The Stapleton Collection/The Bridgeman Art Library; 11T, Courtesy of Everett Collection; 11B, © KRT/PressLink/Newscom; 12, © Richard W. Rodriguez/Fort Worth Star-Telegram/MCT/Newscom; 13L, © UPI Photo/Bill Greenblatt/Newscom; 13C, © blickwinkel/Rainer/Alamy; 13R, © Mark A. Johnson/Alamy; 14, © BIOS/Peter Arnold Inc.; 15T, © Faith A. Uridel/kimballstock; 15B, © Shirley Fernandez/Paulette Johnson; 16, © Vicky Kasala/Photodisc/Alamy; 17T, © Paulette Johnson; 17B, © Pat Doyle/Corbis; 18, © Stefan Haehnsen/dpaphotos/Newscom; 19TL, © AP Images/Aaron Favila; 19BL, © AP Images/Aaron Favila; 19R, © Alley Cat Productions/Brand X/Corbis; 20, © Yoshio Tomii/SuperStock; 21T, © Grossemy Vanessa/Belpress/Andia/digital railroad; 21B, © Sharon Montrose/The Image Bank/Getty Images; 22, © age fotostock /SuperStock; 23, © pixshots/Shutterstock; 24, Courtesy of Ruth DeFranco/www.dogonahog.org; 25, © Courtesy of Ruth DeFranco/www.dogonahog.org; 26, © MGM/The Kobal Collection/Tracy Bennett; 27L, © Charles Harris/AdMedia/Newscom; 27R, © Walt Disney Pictures/Photofest; 28, © pixshots/Shutterstock; 29, © Dave King/Dorling Kindersley; 31, © Eric Isselée/Shutterstock; 32, © Eric Isselée/Shutterstock.

Publisher: Kenn Goin
Editorial Director: Adam Siegel
Creative Director: Spencer Brinker
Photo Researcher: Amy Dunleavy
Design: Dawn Beard Creative

Library of Congress Cataloging-in-Publication Data

Lunis, Natalie.
  Chihuahua : señor tiny / by Natalie Lunis.
    p. cm. — (Little dogs rock!)
  Includes bibliographical references and index.
  ISBN-13: 978-1-59716-743-7 (library binding)
  ISBN-10: 1-59716-743-6 (library binding)
  1. Chihuahua (Dog breed)—Juvenile literature. I. Title.

  SF429.C45L86 2009
  636.76—dc22
                    2008030828

For more information, write to Bearport Publishing Company, Inc., 101 Fifth Avenue, Suite 6R, New York, New York 10003. Printed in the United States of America.

10 9 8 7 6 5 4 3 2 1

Contents

Little Dog, Big Hero

One-year-old Booker West was playing in his grandparents' backyard in Masonville, Colorado. His grandfather was keeping an eye on him as he splashed his hands in a little birdbath. So was Zoey (ZOH-ee)—the family's fluffy Chihuahua (chuh-WHA-wha).

Suddenly, Zoey heard a rattling sound. She knew the sound meant that there was a rattlesnake nearby—and that it was about to attack. Zoey rushed to protect the little boy. She jumped in between him and the snake. Instead of biting Booker, the rattlesnake bit Zoey on the head. The little dog had saved the boy's life.

Zoey watching Booker playing in his grandparents' birdbath

Rattlesnakes are among the most dangerous snakes in the United States. Many kinds rattle their tails as a warning before biting.

Tiny but Tough

Rattlesnake bites can be deadly for an adult person. They are even more dangerous for a dog like Zoey that weighs only five pounds (2.2 kg).

Zoey was lucky. Her family rushed her to a **veterinarian** right after the attack. The medicines that she got from the doctor saved her life. After a few days, the little Chihuahua was almost back to normal.

▲ **Zoey, Booker, and Booker's grandparents after the rescue**

During an interview, Booker's grandmother told reporters that little dogs don't often get credit for being heroes. As Zoey proved, however, a tiny Chihuahua can be just as brave and loyal as any big dog.

Zoey

Chihuahuas are the smallest of all dog **breeds**. Most of these tiny dogs weigh less than six pounds (2.7 kg).

After she was bitten, Zoey's head ▶ swelled to the size of a grapefruit. Once the swelling went down, she was left with a scar on her head.

A Dog of Ancient Mexico

Chihuahuas aren't only the smallest of dog breeds—they are also one of the oldest. Their history goes back about 1,000 years to ancient Mexico. There, the **Toltecs** and other groups that came after them, such as the **Aztecs**, built great cities. They also raised small dogs that were the **ancestors** of today's Chihuahuas.

These clay figures of Chihuahua ancestors were made more than 1,000 years ago.

The ancestor of the Chihuahua was called the Techichi (teh-CHEE-chee) in ancient Mexico.

In the early 1500s, soldiers from Spain invaded the land of the Aztecs and destroyed their cities. Little is known about what happened to the small dogs of ancient Mexico for the next 300 years or so. Then, in 1850, the dogs were rediscovered—and began their rise to **fame**.

The people who lived in ancient Mexico before the Spanish arrived built huge pyramids. Artwork showing the Techichi has been found in some of them.

◀ Montezuma (*mon*-teh-ZOO-muh) II, the last Aztec emperor, ruled ancient Mexico from 1502 to 1520. He may have had hundreds of Chihuahua-like dogs living in his palace.

Becoming a Big Name

Chihuahua is a state in northern Mexico. In the mid-1800s, people in local markets there started selling little dogs to visiting Americans. The dogs, which came to be known as Chihuahuas, had been found living in ancient **ruins**. They were the **descendants** of the dogs of ancient Mexico.

▲ **Chihuahua is the largest state in Mexico. The state's capital city is also called Chihuahua.**

After their arrival in the United States, Chihuahuas started to catch on as pets. They became even more popular in the 1930s and 1940s. During these years, **Latin American** movie stars and bandleaders were a big hit with U.S. audiences. Several of the **glamorous** stars loved Chihuahuas and were often photographed with their pint-sized pets.

Bandleader Xavier Cugat ▶ was known as the Rhumba King. He sometimes held a Chihuahua in one hand and his baton in the other as he led his musicians.

¡Yo Quiero Taco Bell!

The Chihuahua's popularity soared again in the late 1990s. That's when a Chihuahua named Gidget starred in a series of commercials for the restaurant chain Taco Bell.

▲ **In this Taco Bell ad, the Chihuahua is saying, "I want Taco Bell!"**

Staying in the Spotlight

Today, as in the 1930s and 1940s, Chihuahuas are often spotted with **celebrities**. One of the most famous Chihuahua owners is dog trainer Cesar Millan—who is also known as the Dog Whisperer. Other well-known Chihuahua owners include Madonna, Rosie O'Donnell, Hilary Duff, and Jennifer Lopez.

Cesar Millan's Chihuahua is named Coco. She often helps Cesar train other dogs.

Chihuahuas aren't just a big hit with television and music stars, however. Everyday dog owners love them, too. Year after year, the Chihuahua ranks in the list of the top 20 most popular dog breeds, according to the **American Kennel Club**.

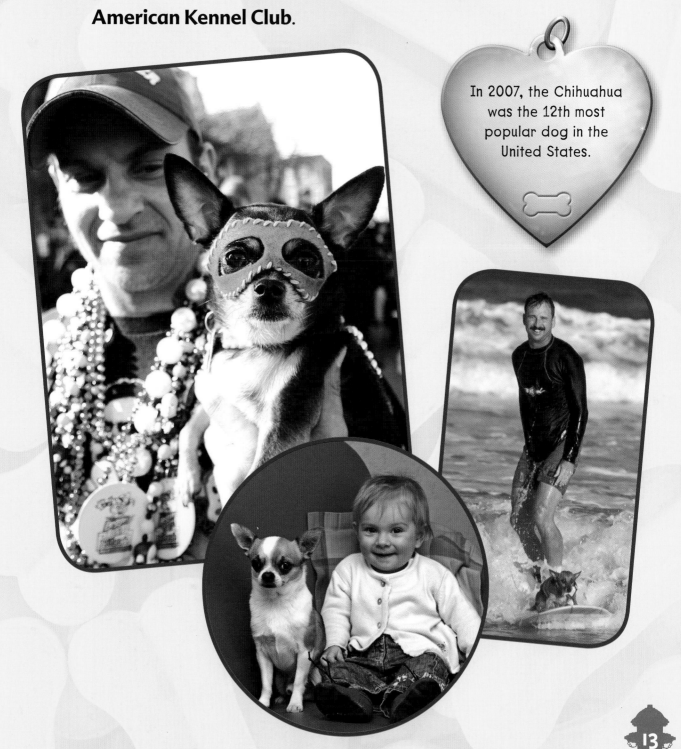

In 2007, the Chihuahua was the 12th most popular dog in the United States.

Coats of Many Colors

When most people picture a Chihuahua, they see a tiny dog with big eyes and big ears. Yet Chihuahuas get their one-of-a-kind look from more than just their little bodies and sweet faces. Their **coats** and their colors also help make them special.

Chihuahuas are known for their big eyes and ears.

Chihuahuas can be long-haired or short-haired. They also come in a huge range of colors. They can be solid tan, white, cream, red, gold, silver, brown, or black. Or they can have coats with different colored markings. In fact, Chihuahuas come in every color pattern that is known for dogs.

A short-haired (left) and two long-haired Chihuahuas

The color of some Chihuahuas' coats is called blue. The color is not really blue, however. It is actually bluish-gray.

◄ A "blue" Chihuahua puppy

A Perfect Pet

Because of their small size, Chihuahuas are easy to care for in many ways. They can live in an apartment or a house with a very small yard and still get enough exercise. Also, they don't eat much, especially compared to big dogs.

Like all dogs, Chihuahuas need to be walked. However, they don't need to walk as far as big dogs to get enough exercise.

In general, small dogs live longer than big dogs. Healthy Chihuahuas usually live for 15 years or more.

Many Chihuahua owners love carrying their little, lightweight pets around town—even into stores and offices. Others love to cuddle their Chihuahuas in their laps. That's not something you can do with a larger dog, like a golden retriever or a Great Dane!

◀ Chihuahuas are easy to groom—though the long-haired ones need more care than the short-haired ones.

It's not hard for ▶ Chihuahua owners to bring their small pets with them wherever they go.

Handle with Care

A Chihuahua's small size can make it easier to handle than many other kinds of dogs. Yet in some ways, Chihuahua owners need to be especially careful with their **delicate** pets.

Chihuahuas can be easily **injured** if they fall. So they need help getting down from sofas and chairs. They also should not be handled by small children, who might drop them.

Chihuahuas get cold easily. Many owners dress them in sweaters or coats when the temperature drops.

Chihuahuas should not be left alone outdoors. Wild animals such as skunks or raccoons might attack them. Sometimes even big dogs attack Chihuahuas or other little dogs, because they think of them as **prey**.

Some people can't help dressing up their tiny friends just for fun!

Tiny Puppies

All puppies are small, but Chihuahua puppies are especially tiny. Most weigh only three or four ounces (85 or 113 g) when they are born—about as much as an apple. By the time they are a month old, they weigh about one pound (453 g).

Many Chihuahua puppies start out with floppy ears. However, as they grow into adults, their ears start to stand up straight.

Larger kinds of puppies, such as golden retrievers or collies, are usually ready to leave their mothers at the age of eight weeks. However, Chihuahua puppies need to stay with their mothers at least a week longer so that they can build up their strength. Then they are ready to become part of a human family.

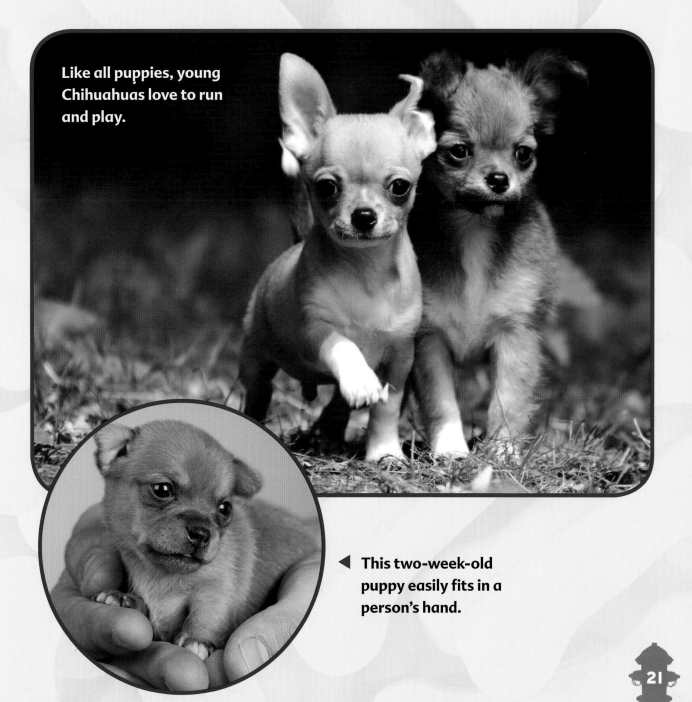

Like all puppies, young Chihuahuas love to run and play.

◄ **This two-week-old puppy easily fits in a person's hand.**

Learning to Get Along

Chihuahuas are intelligent. Yet like all dogs, they need **training** to learn good manners. For example, they need to learn not to bark too much.

One thing Chihuahuas don't need to learn is how to get along with their owners or with other Chihuahuas. That's because they seem to naturally **bond** with their human families and with other dogs just like themselves. However, careful training can help the little dogs get along with all kinds of creatures—including cats, big dogs, and people other than their owners.

▲ **A Chihuahua and a Great Dane**

Chihuahuas often challenge big dogs. Owners need to be careful that the larger dog doesn't hurt the Chihuahua.

Happy to Help

Chihuahuas bring fun and friendship into the lives of their owners. Some also form a close bond with children and adults in schools, hospitals, and nursing homes. These friendly and well-behaved Chihuahuas work as **therapy dogs**. They cheer up people who are sad, lonely, or sick. One of the flashiest therapy dogs around is a long-haired Chihuahua from Ohio named Bear.

▲ In 2004, Bear won an award from the Ohio Veterinary Medical Association. He was named "Outstanding Therapy Animal."

One day, Bear's owner saw a little remote-control motorcycle in a store. She bought it and spent four months teaching Bear to ride it. Now everyone smiles and laughs when Bear roars into the room wearing his little leather jacket, hat, and sunglasses.

When Bear visits schools and libraries, he helps children become better readers. He lies on the floor and listens while they read aloud.

◄ **Bear's owner calls the little dog's motorcycle the "Chihuahua chopper."**

Star Quality

Chihuahuas attract attention whenever they step out. They have also become famous by appearing on the movie screen.

The most well-known movie Chihuahua is Bruiser in *Legally Blonde* (2001). Bruiser goes just about everywhere with his owner, a law student played by Reese Witherspoon.

In *Legally Blonde*, Bruiser is played by a Chihuahua named Moonie. In the **sequel**, *Legally Blonde 2: Red, White, and Blonde* (2003), Bruiser's mother appears and is played by Gidget—the Chihuahua that starred in the Taco Bell commercials.

▲ **Moonie and Reese Witherspoon in a scene from *Legally Blonde***

In the movie *Beverly Hills Chihuahua* (2008), a Chihuahua named Chloe (KLOH-ee) is taken on a trip to Mexico by her owner's niece. While she is there, Chloe is "dognapped" and has to find a way to escape and get back home to California.

Of course, Bruiser and Chloe have adventures that can happen only in movies. In one important way, however, they are just like real Chihuahuas. They are little dogs with big personalities and many fans.

Chihuahuas at a Glance

Weight:	2–8 pounds (1–3.6 kg)
Height at Shoulder:	6–9 inches (15–23 cm)
Coat Hair:	Short or long
Colors:	Some are solid tan, cream, brown, red, gold, white, black, blue, or silver; others are a combination of these colors
Country of Origin:	Mexico
Life Span:	About 15 years
Personality:	Alert, bold, and loyal; cautious around strangers; not afraid of challenging bigger dogs

Best in Show

What makes a great Chihuahua? Every owner knows that his or her dog is special. Judges in dog shows, however, look very carefully at a Chihuahua's appearance and behavior. Here are some of the things they look for:

large ears stand straight up when dog is alert and spread slightly to the side when dog is resting

skull has a round, apple dome shape

tail is carried up or in a curl over the back with the tip just barely touching the back

muzzle is short and slightly pointed

Behavior:
should be alert

Ideal Weight:
2–6 pounds (1–3 kg)

small, dainty feet

Glossary

American Kennel Club (uh-MER-uh-kuhn KEN-uhl KLUHB) a national organization that is involved in many activities having to do with dogs, including collecting information about dog breeds, registering purebred dogs, and setting rules for dog shows

ancestors (AN-sess-turz) relatives who lived a long time ago

Aztecs (AZ-teks) people of a Native American empire in Mexico, during the 1400s through the early 1500s

bond (BOND) to form a close friendship or connection

breeds (BREEDZ) kinds of dogs that look very much alike

celebrities (suh-LEB-ruh-teez) famous people

coats (KOHTS) the fur on dogs or other animals

delicate (DEL-uh-kuht) easily hurt

descendants (di-SEND-uhnts) living things that are related to other living things from the past

fame (FAYM) being well known

glamorous (GLAM-ur-uhss) very exciting and attractive

injured (IN-jurd) hurt

Latin American (LAT-uhn uh-MER-uh-kuhn) having to do with the people and cultures of Mexico, Central America, and South America

prey (PRAY) animals that are hunted for food

ruins (ROO-inz) what is left of something that has collapsed or been destroyed

sequel (SEE-kwuhl) a movie or book that is created to continue the story of another movie or book

therapy dogs (THER-uh-pee DAWGZ) dogs that visit places such as hospitals to cheer people up and make them feel more comfortable

Toltecs (TOHL-teks) people of a Native American empire in Mexico, during the 900s through the 1100s

training (TRAYN-ing) being taught to do certain things

veterinarian (*vet*-ur-uh-NER-ee-uhn) a doctor who takes care of dogs and other animals

Bibliography

Andrews, Barbara J. *Chihuahua.* Allenhurst, NJ: Kennel Club Books (2006).

Coile, D. Caroline. *The Chihuahua Handbook.* Hauppauge, NY: Barron's (2000).

Miller, Richard, with Diane Morgan. *Chihuahuas (Animal Planet Pet Care Library).* Neptune City, NJ: T.F.H. Publications, Inc. (2006).

Walker, Joan Hustace. *The Everything Chihuahua Book: A Complete Guide to Raising, Training, and Caring for Your Chihuahua.* Avon, MA: Adams Media (2006).

Read More

Gagne, Tammy. *Chihuahuas.* Mankato, MN: Capstone Press (2009).

Gray, Susan H. *Chihuahuas.* Chanhassen, MN: Child's World (2007).

Stone, Lynn M. *Chihuahuas.* Vero Beach, FL: Rourke (2005).

Learn More Online

To learn more about Chihuahuas, visit
www.bearportpublishing.com/LittleDogsRock

Index

About the Author

Natalie Lunis has written many science and nature books for children. She lives in the Hudson River Valley, just north of New York City.